THE
BLUFFER'S® GUIDE
TO
ASTROLOGY
& FORTUNE TELLING

ALEXANDER C. RAE

Oval Books

Published by Oval Books
335 Kennington Road
London SE11 4QE
United Kingdom

Telephone: +44 (0)20 7582 7123
Fax: +44 (0)20 7582 1022
E-mail: info@ovalbooks.com
Web site: www.ovalbooks.com

Published by Ravette Publishing, 1988
New Edition 1992, reprinted 1993

Published by Oval Books, 2000

New Edition 2005

Series Editor – Anne Tauté

Cover designer – Vicki Towers
Cover image – © Dave G. Houser/Corbis
Printer – Gopsons Papers Ltd.
Producer – Oval Projects Ltd.

The Bluffer's® Guides series is based
on an original idea by Peter Wolfe.

The Bluffer's Guide®, The Bluffer's
Guides®, Bluffer's®, and Bluff Your
Way® are Registered Trademarks.

ISBN-13: 978-1-903096-37-6
ISBN-10: 1-903096-37-5

CONTENTS

Introduction	5
Interpretation	6
The Golden Rules	6
Astrology	10
The Theory	11
Popular Astrology	11
Having Fun with Astrology	16
The Signs	19
The Elements	21
Predictions	22
Chinese Astrology	24
The Tarot	26
Picking the Pack	27
Reading the Cards	28
The Major or Grand Arcana	28
The Minor Arcana	32
Face Cards	33
Numbers	34
Layouts	36
Having Fun with the Tarot	37
I Ching	38
Casting the Hexagram	39
The Yarrow Stalk Method	39
The Coin Method	40
Interpretation	41
Jung and I Ching	42
Palmistry	43

Technical Terms   44
The Technique   45
  The Mounts   47
  The Lines   48

Runes   50

Oneiromancy   51
Interpretation   53

Phrenology   55
Interpretation   56

Metoposcopy   58

Molescopy   60
General Rules   61

Geomancy   62

INTRODUCTION

In most areas of human endeavour bluffi
way out – a method of artificially appea
edgeable. In fortune telling it is a way of
there are those who would suggest (rathe
that it is nothing but a stylised, ritualise
bluffing from beginning to end.

Even if you believe that it is not all total
it is worthwhile remembering a fundamenta
is easier to persuade other people that you
the future than to actually do it.

There are many in-built advantages for the
in this activity. Even the most sensible people
quite prepared to believe in the most unlikely me
People rush to have their future revealed by gy
when they wouldn't think of asking advice from an
whose main source of income is selling clothes peg

What follows is a reasonably comprehensive summ
of Astrology and related forms of predictive scien
with enough details to pass yourself off as an expe
and to allow you to charge extortionate fees for you
readings.

Each section has a rating for obscurity, for artistic
interpretation and for technical merit. The higher the
obscurity rating, the easier it is for novice bluffers to
pass themselves off as experts.

The artistic interpretation mark shows whether the
form of augury is easy to interpret. In practice this
means having the least amount of details to remember
and the most clues to help you make it up as you go
along. The technical merit shows you how complicated
the science seems to the general public – the greater
the degree of apparent complexity the greater the
kudos for having mastered the art.

NTERPRETATION

uffing is so important in the telling of fortunes that
othsayers have invented their own special word for
. They call it 'interpretation'.

Don't worry about this art. It is all delightfully simple
you just remember the Seven Golden Rules. Learn
hese by heart and you are three quarters of the way
owards being not just an astrologer, but a clairvoyant.

The Golden Rules

1. No-one really wants to know their future. People
   consult Astrology, cards, etc., because they are worried
   about the future. They want to be reassured. They
   don't want to worry more. Even if you really think
   they will go bankrupt or that their romance is
   doomed, don't tell them that. The trick is to tell them
   what they want to hear, without seeming to do so.

2. Insist that the querent (seeker after knowledge and
   truth) asks you a specific question. As he or she
   speaks, watch carefully. They will tell you in their
   question and in their body language what they
   want to hear. Don't blurt out the answer immediately, though. Throw in a couple of meaningless
   predictions first and then slip it in casually after six
   minutes when they are beginning to get worried
   that you weren't going to mention it. This allows
   you to build up the tension.

3. Give the impression that you know more than you
   are prepared to say. Then when someone comes

back and says 'But you never mentioned that I was going to be struck by lightning,' you can always say "Well I wondered when I saw Saturn in Virgo (or whatever is suitable) but I didn't want to worry you." He or she might not believe you, but would seldom say so to your face.

4. Take a keen interest in the science of statistical possibility. Always try to predict something with at least a 50/50 chance of happening. If a good looking 18-year-old girl asks 'Will I get married in the next year?' you can answer "Well certainly in the next two years."

5. Pick as complicated a method of prediction as you can handle. With a really complex system, for every positive statement you make you can always find another element of the prediction that reverses it. This is very handy when things go wrong. For example, you can say "I know I said that with the Sun in Sagittarius this was the time to take risks but you really should have remembered that I also told you Pluto squared to Saturn would make activities like hang gliding unpredictable."

   If you have mentioned 50 or 60 different aspects and planetary positions they won't be able to remember whether you actually mentioned that Pluto was squared to Saturn, and certainly not what you said it meant.

6. Make as many predictions as you can think of (mostly small things that are nowhere near significant enough to be remembered). Mention as wide a variety of subjects as possible (in a vague way) – travel, career developments, minor ailments, tall

dark strangers, that sort of thing. Then a month later, when they get a promotion or they lose their jobs, all they will remember is that you mentioned something about their career and they will presume that you have accurately predicted it. Never be too specific. For instance, you can say "You may receive a great honour in the next five years" not "You will win the Miss World Competition next Thursday".

7. Explain what you are doing as you go along. Use as many jargon terms as possible (make them up if necessary) to make it look as if you have some basis for any obvious statement you make. For instance, when reading the palm of a six-foot-three boxer with a broken nose it might seem a bit obvious to say "You are inclined to express yourself physically". But if you say "Look at the development of your Plain of Mars. That means you are inclined to externalise your aggressions..." he will be impressed. On the other hand many expert bluffers would not tell a six-foot-three boxer anything that might possibly be misconstrued as insulting, so it might be better to suggest that his hand shows he is really a gentle, misunderstood kind of person.

These simple rules apply to every method of the augury and can be used with devastating effect. They vary widely from simple make-it-up-as-you-go-along methods like **Skrying** (always call it skrying – crystal ball gazing just sounds silly) to complicated 'sciences' like **Astrology**, where you have to go through hours of tortuous mathematics before you start making it up as you go along.

8

If you are not totally confident in the world of bluffing it is best to choose an obscure method of divination. Pick a popular science and you will be rubbing shoulders with some of the best, most experienced bluffers in the world. It is still possible to get away with it by accusing your competitors of being charlatans and viciously denigrating everything they say. This is vital because the nonsense you make up will be totally different from the nonsense they have made up and the easiest way to maintain your credibility is to attack theirs. But remember they will probably be trying to do the same thing to you.

So it is better to use a totally obscure method which no-one feels threatened by. For instance, as far as we know there are no professional exponents of **Alectryomancy** (predicting the future from the eating patterns of sacred chickens) and there are only two registered **Cephalomancists** (people who can forecast events based on the shape of the skull of a donkey). These particular forms of augury won't suit everyone of course. There are people who don't own a donkey, or have an allergy to sacred chickens – but there are plenty more.

"Predictive sciences", "prognosticative powers" or even "oracular sensitivity" are all terms which mean fortune telling, and somehow sound better. Use them regularly. As a general rule use the most significant description (i.e., the longest words). Don't 'read tea leaves' – use "tasseographic augury".

ASTROLOGY

At first sight Astrology would seem the perfect medium for a beginner because:

a) It is a science, with hours of hard (impressive looking) work to elicit the simplest facts

b) It is immensely complicated with the position of the sun and nine planets and the relationship of the planets to each other all having to be taken into account

c) It has gained such respect that there are now correspondence courses to teach you the basics.

The fact is: it doesn't just seem complicated – it *is* complicated. Hours of mind-crunching toil are needed to work out the simplest facts and if you are the sort of person prepared to do that you will never make a real bluffer. Don't be tempted into thinking you can cut corners either. Because it's so popular you cannot move without coming across an 'expert'. Make the slightest slip and it's "Did you take an hour off to allow for British Summer Time?" and "Are you sure you computed Sidereal Time correctly?"

It is far better to be the know-all when someone else is trying to impress, and all the time have a bag of Runes or a Tarot pack in your pocket ready to win the trust of the disillusioned audience.

However, Astrology is so much part of modern day augury that you need at least the appearance of a deep knowledge. You can then persuade people that although you are an expert in Astrology you gave it all up because you found **Ichthyomancy** (predictions based on the entrails of fish) so much more effective.

The Theory

The theory of Astrology is based on the fact that the waxing and waning of the Moon has an effect on the moods of humans. (Whether this really has been proved doesn't matter. No-one but a lunatic would argue.) Therefore, astrologers assert, the movement of much larger heavenly bodies – the sun and the eight planets – will also have an effect on different aspects of our lives.

So astrologers carefully compute the position of all the planets at the exact moment of birth – a natal chart. Why the moment of birth is important is mysteriously glossed over. In fact it would be far more scientific to suggest that the moment of conception would be the time when the influence of the planets would be most significant. But it has to be admitted that lying in bed with a stop watch trying to work out the exact moment of conception might just take some of the romance out of life.

This needn't prevent you mentioning the fact if anyone tries to show off the fruits of their Academy of Astrological Science's Diploma – Part II.

Popular Astrology

It is vital to dismiss the astrological predictions presented in the 'popular press'. Look surprised and/or smile condescendingly if anyone admits that they 'read their stars every day'.

Any arguments on this score can be crushed quite easily by pointing out that if one believed in this form of prediction a twelfth of the world's population should be 'prepared to receive a letter from an uncle you didn't know you had' on the same day. This would imply that one or two head-hunters in the Borneo jungle who have had no contact with the outside world are in for a big surprise that day.

You then explain that what people call their 'Sign of the Zodiac' is merely the sign that the Sun was in at the moment of their birth. Of equal importance is the position of:

a) their **Ascendant** – what sign was coming up over the horizon at the moment of birth;

b) their **Mid-Heaven** or **Medium Coeli** (the same thing but sounds much better in Latin) – what sign was directly overhead at birth; and

c) the **Planets** – Moon, Mercury, Jupiter, Mars, Venus, Saturn, Pluto, Uranus and Neptune.

The Ascendant

All 12 signs of the zodiac come over the horizon every day so you need to know the exact moment of your birth to decide which sign was on the horizon at that instant. With the sign changing a degree every four minutes, half an hour out can make a tremendous difference. It therefore needs to be calculated very carefully using an **ephemeris** (a book of charts with the positions of all the planets) and pages of calculations. This is just too much trouble for the average bluffer. As it decides what your inner nature is like, just pick one you think suits the situation.

The Mid Heaven or the Medium Coeli

This also needs careful calculation and the purpose it serves is so vague that it definitely isn't worth the trouble. It covers the personality that you present to the world so everyone should know that already.

The Planets

You need at least a vague idea of what the planets signify and what aspects of your life they are supposed to rule. It is also important to recognise the symbol used to signify the planets. For instance if you were writing out your interpretation of a natal chart never write the word 'Mars' when you can draw the little circle with the arrow sticking out of the top. Not only does it prove you know the subject, it means that clients constantly have to ask you what all the little signs mean, which makes you indispensable.

Here is a brief description of each.

The Sun ☉
This is the one thing everyone knows. If someone says they are a Virgo it means that the Sun was in the sign of Virgo when they were born. It only changes once a month but no-one can make up their mind when it is. Astrologers put the **cusp** (the day when it moves from one house to another) at anything between the 19th and 24th of each month. The sun sign really is important, strongly influencing the way you lead your life, but never admit this to anyone. Because everyone knows about it, it is best to belittle its importance in favour of Neptune or whatever your favourite planet is. Key word: life-force.

The Moon ☾

This deals with all sorts of mysterious things like motherhood and nurture. As it follows its regular pattern of waxing and waning, it also covers habits. Always talk about intuition when you talk about the moon. (Intuition should be brought into at least three out of every four sentences in every form of fortune telling.) Key word: intuition.

Mercury ☿

Mercury, the messenger of the gods, deals with all forms of communications and travel. Mercury moves very quickly through the heavens, which is why so many astrological predictions have mysterious letters and interesting journeys cropping up. Whenever you talk about Mercury it's worthwhile mentioning that though most people think of it as a 'male' deity the symbolism is purely female. The sign of Mercury is the sign for Venus with the crescent Moon on top. Key word: communications.

Venus ♀

As everyone remembers, Venus was the goddess of Love so the movements of this planet about the heavens have an intimate influence on our love/sex life. It is therefore the planet that people take the most interest in. Key word: sex.

Mars ♂

The arrow is the clue. As war is not so popular as it once was astrologers usually try to make the God of War palatable by talking about self-assertiveness and energy. Key word: violence.

Jupiter ♃

As king of the gods, Jupiter rules all the important things like ambition and career. Therefore he is quite often as welcome as Venus. Key word: career.

Saturn ♄

There's got to be one trouble maker. The Romans let Saturn rule the underworld and he's not much cheerier nowadays. Astrologers talk about restrictions and discipline but Saturn is really about luck – and most of its bad. Key word: fate.

The New Planets ♅ ♆ ♇

When the old astrologers apportioned the duties for all the planets, they didn't know about Uranus, Neptune and Pluto (no-one noticed Uranus until 1781, and Pluto was only spotted hiding behind Neptune in 1931). By that time they had naturally given all the interesting duties to the planets they knew about and were really scraping the bottom of the barrel to find something for the last three to influence. What self-respecting planet would govern 'regeneration' (Pluto) or 'refinement through dissolution' (Neptune)? People are really only interested in things like sex (Venus) and violence (Mars).

This means that you can make up your own interpretation for these planets without conflicting with any traditional astrological beliefs. Modern popular astrologers are inclined to pay a great amount of attention to them, just because no-one is in a position to argue with their interpretation.

It is often worth using the alternative name for Uranus – Herschel. Not only is it handy for confusing people, it also sounds more seemly to say "I find

Herschel particularly interesting" than "I find Uranus particularly interesting." It is named after Sir William Herschel (the man who discovered it) just as Pluto was named after its discoverer (better known as a close friend of Mickey Mouse).

Having Fun with Astrology

The other detail about these three vague, new planets worth using to effect is that because they are so far away they take an inordinate amount of time to move from one house to another. This little known fact is used in:

Gambit 1 – The old '**Pluto in Leo**' trick.

If you find you are facing someone who thinks they know a bit about Astrology (i.e., someone who has had a natal chart drawn up and knows where their planets were situated at the moment they were born) just look at them thoughtfully, then say "You must have Pluto in ..." and tell them what house Pluto was in at the moment of their birth.

This isn't as difficult as it sounds. Pluto only changes house about every 15 years so you know that anyone born before the Second World War will probably be Pluto in Pisces. Someone born between 1939 and 1956 has Pluto in Leo, and for a someone born between 1957 and 1971 you can say Pluto in Libra.

If they seem amazed at your ability to see the influence of a relatively minor planet in their personality be sure to have a suitable reason for your deduction ready. A good one is "I always find that Pluto in

Leo people instinctively know when someone is telling them the truth". This both flatters and implies that you must be telling the truth or the querent would have already seen through your pretences.

The same trick works with Uranus and Neptune (Uranus changes house every 14 years and Neptune every seven years) but beware of trying to remember too many details – if you learnt all that you would be as well learning Astrology properly.

Should someone happen to know about how slow moving the new planets are, the official line to take is that they influence a whole generation impersonally, rather than having a traumatic effect on an individual.

Gambit 2 – The '**I know what sign of the zodiac you are**' opening.

This can only be used sparingly. It involves going round a group of people telling them all what their Sun Signs are. There are two ways of doing this:

a) You can learn the attributes of all the signs and then apply them to what you know about the personality of each person and systematically work out the correct sign (not recommended), or

b) You can ask them all some time before when their birthday is (they'll never remember), work out what everyone's Sun sign is and then just rhyme them off like a parrot (highly recommended).

The effect is stunning. It doesn't matter if there are some you don't know. Take a guess (you have a one in 12 chance). If you happen to get any wrong there are at least a couple of ways of covering your mistake.

1. Ask what date in the month the person's birthday is, then laugh gently and say "Oh yes. Getting near the cusp" (between the 19th and 24th of the month, but if you are working with people who don't seem to know too much, you can use it to cover any date in the month). If you hear astrologers use the phrase 'near the cusp' you know it is their way of saying "I will not be held responsible for any statement that I shall now make" – the astrologers' form of contractual small print.

2. Ask the person involved what their Ascendant is. If they know it, just smile. Anyone who knows his or her Ascendant is probably an expert (i.e., someone who has read a book on the subject). If they don't know, the world is your oyster. If you've just guessed that someone's Sun Sign is Virgo and they inform you that it is really Aries there is no need even to look embarrassed. Just say "But I bet that your Ascendant is in Virgo." (This can be extended – see **Gambit 3**.) Then explain that because the Ascendant shows the real inner personality it was your sensitive, psychic nature that saw through to their real inner nature. Try not to laugh when you're saying this.

Gambit 3 – The '**I know your Ascendant**' ruse.

This is like the Sun sign ploy, except that you tell everyone what sign their Ascendant is – their Rising Sign. As virtually no-one knows what their Ascendant is, it has the advantage that they can't prove you wrong.

Just go round the room giving each person the sign

that you think most suitable (i.e., one you can talk about sensibly if they ask you what effect this has on them). This can be great fun. For instance you always tell the most macho males they're really Virgos and tell the drunks that they're Pisces.

The real worry is that you may create enough interest for them to go out of their way to find out where their Ascendant really is and prove you wrong. To guard against this take careful details of where and when they were born (the latitude and longitude are both needed) and tell them that you will work it out for them. Don't do it of course. Just come back a week later and tell them you worked out their natal chart and you had guessed correctly. It works every time.

You may have to give a description of the sort of character this will give them. You probably won't be able to remember details of all the signs so it is worthwhile swotting up on two or three special signs to cover all eventualities – say Gemini (for the bubbly characters), Taurus (for the dull ones) and Cancer (for the ones you can't make your mind up about).

The Signs

The one thing that puts everyone off learning Astrology is the fact that when you want to find out what a specific sign means all the books give you are a jumble of seemingly unconnected key words. What these books are purposely hiding is that each of these signs is supposed to describe a specific personality type. You are supposed to recognise an 'Aries type' or a Libran.

So forget all the key words. Just associate each sign with a person and then just use the words you would use to describe that person whenever you have to describe the effects of the sign. There should be someone you know who is a typical Geminian for instance. They don't actually have to be a Geminian, in fact it's unlikely that they will be. They just need to typify the astrologer's idea of a Geminian.

Don't push this too far. Remember it is just the general personality traits we are talking about. Don't start insisting that all Taurians are bald and knobbly-kneed but obsessive just because your friend George is.

In case you don't have 12 friends with different personalities here is an idea of what jobs might suit each sign of the zodiac.

Aries – Assertive, aggressive, enthusiastic, selfish – A double-glazing salesman.

Taurus – Possessive, stable, patient, greedy, demanding – An accountant.

Gemini – Communicative, witty, cunning, unstable – The person who organises games at parties.

Cancer – Protective, nurturing, defensive, touchy, moody – A nurse.

Leo – Impressive, self confident, arrogant, pompous, patronising – A Member of Parliament.

Virgo – Perfectionist, fastidious, pedantic, precise – A maiden aunt.

Libra – Co-operative, diplomatic, peaceable, frivolous – A Bluffer's Guide author.

Scorpio – Intense, fanatical, dramatic, mysterious, destructive – A mass murderer.

Sagittarius – Adventurous, freedom loving, wise, jovial, tactless – A chat show host.

Capricorn – Disciplined, careful, stern, mean, callous – A traffic warden.

Aquarius – Objective, unemotional, detached, scientific – An astrologer.

Pisces – Imaginative, impractical, impressionable, confused – A Bluffer's Guide reader.

The Elements

A handy memory aid for the signs of the zodiac are the Elements. Each sign comes under the influence of an Element – Earth, Fire, Water or Air. So if you can remember that Taurus, Virgo and Capricorn are earth signs you will immediately remember that the essence of all three signs is that they are solid, dependable and dull.

In the same way Aries, Leo and Sagittarius are fire signs (assertive, energetic and pushy): Gemini, Libra and Aquarius are air signs (communicative, lively and a pain) and Cancer, Scorpio and Pisces are water signs (emotional, intuitive and a bit peculiar).

When you think about it they all fit fairly logically with their Element, except for Aquarius which most people want to put in the water signs. Just remember that what looks like water coming from the jar in the symbol is really a flow of words and ideas, and it fits nicely into the air group. Mention this every time Aquarius is discussed and point out that it is the same symbolism as the card 'the Stars' in the Tarot. That always impresses.

It is useful to have a few facts that not many people know about some of the signs. Don't dwell on the one about Gemini and Pisces having split personalities: the two sides of a Geminian personality get on with each other (the twins hold hands) while the Piscean's two characters clash (the fish swim against each other). Everyone knows this and they end up finishing your sentences for you, looking smug.

Instead use the same techniques to find obscure details in the symbolism and make up some unlikely meanings from them. For example, if someone brings up the one about Pisces you say "No. The real symbolism is that the fish come from the sea, the symbol of intuition and the unconscious, so although the fish seem to be swimming away from each other they are communicating telepathically – showing the sensitivity of the Piscean nature." It's nonsense, but no-one will be able to finish your sentence for you.

Predictions

Advanced bluffers who are tempted into prediction using Astrology will have to face the fact that the only way of tackling it is with a computer. With the right software you can work out all the positions and aspects for any date in a matter of minutes. It is also true that people are far more inclined to believe something because they are told it by a computer. Just think how many people pay their phone bills without question. It also allows you to make real predictions. Well, real 'bluffing' predictions.

This is far easier than it sounds. If you are doing predictions for a specific person you should forget about the complicated natal chart and the influence of all the planets, and simply assume that the only influence in their life was their Sun Sign. Then work out the chart for the day that you are predicting.

Take each planet's position and work it out in comparison to the querent's Sun sign. If it is in **Conjunction** (just about the same spot on the chart), **Trine** (at 180 degrees) or **Sextile** (at 60 degrees) to the planet in question, predict something happy.

If it is in **Opposition** (directly opposite) or **Square** (at right angles), predict something bad.

Each planet will affect a different part of your life:

The Sun – General well-being
The Moon – Home life
Mercury – Travel
Venus – Love life
Mars – Argument
Jupiter – Career
Saturn – Luck or Fate

You can even use the symbolism from the sign that the planet is in to help you make up the predictions. So Venus 'trined' to Aries means that your love life will enter a new exciting, active phase, while Venus 'squared' to Scorpio means you will get romantically involved with a mass murderer.

Obscurity rating – 1/10
Artistic interpretation – 7/10
Technical merit – 10/10

CHINESE ASTROLOGY

Less difficult than Astrology is **Chinese Astrology**. A sign in the Chinese Zodiac lasts a year and is named after a limited number of animals so they are pretty easy to remember. Better still, virtually nobody knows anything about it.

There are twelve signs which change every year some time in January or February according to some obscure reference to the Moon. Here is a concise summing up of each personality with the suitable years.

Rat – Charming opportunist.
1936, 1948, 1960, 1972, 1984.

Buffalo – Placid and patient.
1937, 1949, 1961, 1973, 1985.

Tiger – Magnetic leader or rebellious hothead.
1938, 1950, 1962, 1974, 1986.

Rabbit – Peace-loving and affectionate.
1939, 1951, 1963, 1975, 1987.

Dragon – Gifted perfectionist.
1940, 1952, 1964, 1976.

Snake – Elegant snob.
1941, 1953, 1965, 1977.

Horse – Quick witted extrovert.
1942, 1954, 1966, 1978.

Goat – Graceful hedonist.
1943, 1955, 1967, 1979.

Monkey – Intelligent, amusing egotist.
1944, 1956, 1968, 1980.

Rooster – Day-dreamer.
1945, 1957, 1969, 1981.

Dog – Loyal, courageous and faithful.
1946, 1958, 1970, 1982.

Pig – Totally honest and gullible.
1947, 1959, 1971, 1983.

Signs are always attributed one of five elements in the Chinese system, earth, fire, air, water or metal although bluffers have been known to use elements like concrete or tapioca when feeling really silly. Nothing is more fun than telling someone that according to Chinese astrology he or she is a tapioca Gerbil.

Pick a good sign for yourself – a Tiger or a Horse sounds better than a Pig or a Rat. A good technique is to pick out the sign of everyone in the company. If it's someone you don't care for, say something like "You'll be a ferret, I would think. What year were you born?" Then no matter what year they say, smile and say "Oh yes. A plastic ferret" and go on to give them as accurate a summing up of their characters as your imagination will allow.

If anyone starts being clever and points out there is no Hippopotamus or Ferret in Chinese horoscopes, ask if it is Cantonese or Shanghai astrology that they've studied and be an expert on the other one.

Obscurity rating – 8/10
Artistic interpretation – 5/10
Technical merit – 2/10

THE TAROT

Let fortune tellers claim to 'read the future in cards', you will "practise **Cartomancy**".

It is supposed to be possible to tell the future using a normal 52 playing card pack, but bluffers will carry a pack of their favourite **Tarot** cards.

In many ways Tarot is ideal for bluffing. It is by far the best known method of Cartomancy, which gives others confidence and (thanks to countless Hammer Horror films) it carries an air of danger and mystery. Yet Tarot is seldom used for fortune telling other than by professionals.

This can probably be put down to the fact that there are 78 cards which have two separate meanings (depending on whether they are the right way up or reversed) and most people foolishly consider you would have to memorise 156 different interpretations before you could start interpreting (especially when you recall that it is very bad form to look up the meaning of any of the cards in a book).

Experienced bluffers will immediately recognise the potential for practising their own special arts with the Tarot pack.

Tarot has an impressive history. It was brought out of ancient Egypt by the gypsies and is really a method of encoding the secret wisdom of the Pharaohs in symbolic form. Or, if you prefer, the ancient Tarot evolved in the mists of antiquity in India and portrays a secret path of initiation. Both histories have been popular in their time and are usually swallowed without comment.

The facts are that there is no evidence of Tarot being in existence before the 14th century but that doesn't sound very romantic – unless you want to be really obscure and tie it in with the hidden symbolism of the heretical Albigensian sect in France. The average individual will still prefer the one about the gypsies and the Egyptians.

Picking the Pack

A vital factor is choosing the right pack. There are now more types of Tarot packs in circulation than there are people doing Tarot readings. The packs fall into two categories: the traditional and the mystical.

The **traditional** ones all look as if they have been drawn by a talentless seven-year-old. They usually have the names of the cards in French (or other foreign language) and the minimum of clues as to interpretation. The **mystical** ones are beautifully drawn in pretty colours using new, radical symbolism revealed through clairvoyance to someone living in Glastonbury.

If you are confident, choose a traditional pack (such as the Ancient French) and thereafter denigrate modern packs as having lost the authentic Tarot symbolism. Or else choose one of the modern packs and enthuse wildly over the way that designers have recaptured the authentic symbolism of the Tarot which had been lost by the traditional packs.

However, if you choose a modern pack with English titles, always refer to the cards by their French names and vice-versa. It sounds good and swiftly convinces the listeners of your in-depth knowledge of Tarot. This is pretty straightforward except that you have to remember little details like the 'Tower Struck By Lightning' is called the 'Maison De Dieu'. If you're better at Italian, use the Italian names, but it's not quite so classy.

Reading the Cards

The Tarot pack is divided into two groups – the **Major Arcana** and the **Minor Arcana**. Arçana means hidden or secret things, though it has to be admitted that they are not much of a secret now.

The Major or Grand Arcana

The Major Arcana is the 'fun' part of the Tarot. It has 22 cards (numbered 0 to 21 just to be confusing) and contains all the exciting cards – Death, the Devil, the Hanged Man and the Tower Struck By Lightning. These cards are regarded as significant, so if you get any in a reading be sure to say something subtle like "Now that card is from the Grand Arcana and is really significant".

The cards are so full of symbolism that it is pretty easy to guess at a suitable meaning for them. If a card looks quite pleasant and it is upright say something good. If it is reversed say the opposite. If it looks bad say something bad and if it is reversed say something worse. In case there are one or two that are not totally obvious here are a few short suggestions.

0 The Fool/Le Mat/Il Matto

No-one knows anything about this card. Even experts can't decide if it should be first or twenty-second in the Grand Arcana so you are safe to be as vague as possible in interpreting it.

Upright – Here you say something like "It's difficult to give a proper reading for this card. It's the very mystery of the Tarot. But in this case..." and go on to say anything that suits.

Reversed – Who knows?

1 **The Magician/Le Bateleur/Il Bagattelliere**
   Upright – "You can take charge."
   Reversed – "You can't take charge."

2 **The High Priestess/Junon/La Papessa**
   Upright – "Listen to your instincts."
   Reversed – "Don't listen to your instincts."

3 **The Empress/L'Imperatrice/L'Imperatrice**
   Upright – Fertility and abundance.
   Reversed – Sterility or an unwanted pregnancy.

4 **The Emperor/L'Empereur/L'Imperatore**
   Upright – Willpower and ambition.
   Reversed – "You don't have a chance."

5 **The Hierophant/Jupiter/Il Papa**
   Upright – "Listen to good advice."
   Reversed – "Beware of bad advice."

6 **The Lovers/L'Amoureux/Gli Amanti**
   Upright – "An important choice."
   Reversed – "You're going to pick the wrong option."

7 **The Chariot/Le Chariot/Il Carro**
   Upright – "You're really going places."
   Reversed – "Don't move!"

8 **Justice/La Justice/La Giustizia**
   Upright – "You can work things out."
   Reversed – "Get a good lawyer."

9 **The Hermit/L'Ermite/L'Eremita**
Upright – "Take time to think before you act."
Reversed – "If only you'd asked my advice before."

10 **The Wheel of Fortune/La Roue de Fortune/
Ruota della Fortuna**
Upright – "Luckily your future is in the hands of fate."
Reversed – "Your future is in the hands of fate."

11 **Fortitude or Strength/La Force/La Forza**
Upright – "With courage you overcome all opposition."
Reversed – "Run!"

12 **The Hanged Man/Le Pendu/L'Appenzo**
Upright – "It's worth hanging around for a while."
Reversed – "Get a really good lawyer."

13 **Death/La Mort/** (no title).
Upright – "You are liable to undergo a great
change in your life."
Reversed – "Can you pay in cash?"

14 **Temperance/Temperance/La Temperanza**
Upright or Reversed – "Give up drinking."

15 **The Devil/Le Diable/Il Diavolo**
Upright – "Control yourself."
Reversed – "Have you ever thought of seeing an
exorcist?"

16 **The Tower Struck By Lightning/La Maison
De Dieu/La Torre**
Upright – "Being struck by lightning isn't as bad
as you'd think."
Reversed – "Check your house insurance policy."

17 The Stars/L'Etoile/Le Stelle
Upright – "Things are looking up."
Reversed – "Things are due for a downturn".

18 The Moon/La Lune/La Luna
Upright – "Rely on intuition."
Reversed – "Don't think you can rely on intuition."

19 The Sun/Le Soleil/Il Sole
Upright – "I told you it would work out all right."
Reversed – "If only you had asked my advice...."

20 The Judgement/Le Jugement/Il Giudizio
Upright – "You've made it."
Reversed – "I hope you have a good lawyer."

21 The World/Le Monde/Il Mondo
Upright – "The successful completion of a cycle."
Reversed – "Better luck next time."

Don't worry if you can't remember the precise meaning of each card. No-one else does.

Handy Tips

You can always keep people off-balance by insisting that all the things they believed about the Tarot are false. The best one is to say that 13 (Death) is not an unlucky card. Say it means the end of an outmoded phase of their life and an exciting new start. But be sure not to take a post dated cheque for the reading.

In the same vein you can try and persuade everyone that the 'Tower Struck By Lightning' or 'The Devil' are also really lucky cards. It's not true, but it's sometimes fun to give yourself a challenge.

The Minor Arcana

At first sight the Minor Arcana could appear a little bit of a problem. There are 56 cards which of course means 112 possible interpretations and, especially in the traditional packs, there is very little clue as to what they mean. These are in effect just like a normal pack of playing cards except that the suits are Cups, Staves, Swords and Pentacles instead of Hearts, Clubs, Diamonds and Spades.

If you are worried, pick a modern pack with pretty pictures on all the cards and then you won't dry up. For example, the Ancient French pack uses what must be described as an economy of imagination by portraying the 10 of Swords as 10 swords. In the Rider Waite Pack on the other hand, the same card shows a picture of the same 10 swords stuck in someone's back. No prizes for guessing whether that is a lucky card or not.

However the real bluffer despises such cheap tricks. Instead, by using The Bluffer's Patent Numerical Interpretation System you can be confidently producing very complex readings without any artificial aids, in minutes.

The idea is that you just remember what each suit stands for and what each number stands for and then put them together. So:

Cups – This suit covers the querent's love life and emotions. Memory aid: you are inclined to get emotional when you drink.

Staves – This is intellectual activities and career. Memory aid: it is what they used to hit you with at school if you didn't do your lessons.

Swords – All forms of aggression and struggles. You surely don't need a memory aid for that.

Pentacles – This covers all matters to do with money and property. There are some packs that call this suit Coins but insist on calling it Pentacles. It makes it less obvious when you start talking about money.

Face Cards

There are four Face Cards in each suit which are normally interpreted as actual people. So you have:

> **The King** – an older man
> **The Queen** – an older woman
> **The Knight** – a young man
> **The Page** – a young woman.

Therefore you just tie up the card with the suit. Get the King of Pentacles and you say "You'll meet a rich, mature gentleman", or for the Page of Cups, "You'll experience the influence of a beautiful, romantic young woman".

On the other hand if the card is reversed, you are being warned against the influence of the person. A Queen of Swords (reversed) would be a bad tempered, old woman, and the King of Cups (reversed) an older man completely devoid of social graces.

One uncanny fact is that men are statistically far more likely to get the Queen of Swords (reversed) in their reading than the Page of Cups (or even the Page of Pentacles for that matter) and women have been known to have thousands of readings without sight of a Knight of Cups.

Although pages were male, it is generally accepted

that the 'Pages' should represent young women just to even things up. You can make an exception if you are reading the cards for an unattached woman who probably won't object too much to having a three to one chance of meeting a man.

Numbers

The same theory applies to the normal numbered cards except you have to remember the symbolism of the number and then tie it up with the symbolism of the suit. These are pretty simple to remember.

1. The number of the Sun and the Father and shows the matter going ahead positively as planned.

2. The number of the Moon and the Mother and shows that the matter needs intuitive handling.

3. The third member of the trinity is the Child and three therefore signifies a new start. It is ruled by Jupiter so can be linked with careers.

4. Four-square and substantial, four stands for earth and things material (and therefore *money*).

5. There are five senses so five takes on an air of sensuality, selfishness and decadence. Also it is influenced by Mercury and so may have something to do with communications.

6. Six is a bit vague so it is natural that it should be associated with Venus, all romance and idealism.

7. The Bible is full of beasts with seven heads and seven fat and seven thin cows, so seven is traditionally the number of mysticism and religion. It comes under Neptune, the planet of mystery.

8. Eight is Saturn's number and no matter how you look at it that's bad luck. Since people don't want to hear that, talk vaguely about the "flood tide of fate" or suggest that they will have a bit of luck (you don't need to mention it will be bad luck).

9. Nine being nearly 10 is the number of nearly being somewhere; things moving forward to a successful completion. It is ruled by Mars so it is all energy and aggressions.

10. As the highest number, it is sensible to take 10 as the successful completion of any matter and a sign of good luck.

You just tie the two symbols and come up with a meaning for the card. For instance, the Three of Staves (a new start connected with a career and intellect) could be "If you use your brains you could get a new job."

If reversed, the cards keep the same symbolism but it becomes a warning that things could go wrong in that area. So the same card reversed would be "It seems your employers have found out you don't have any brains, so you may be looking for a new job."

The Four of Pentacles (earth and money) would be described as "achieving a situation of financial security". For some reason this card never seems to appear unless it's reversed.

Layouts

There are a number of traditional layouts but you can make up your own as long as you do it consistently and have enough confidence. Just make sure you have a different place for:

a) the recent past;

b) the immediate future;

c) the personal situation;

d) the home;

e) a warning of anything that could hold one back;

f) the ultimate outcome (you can have two or three cards for the ultimate outcome in different parts of the layout so simply choose the one you like the best. Most traditional layouts use this technique).

The best known traditional layouts are:

1. the one based on the **Celtic cross** which answers a specific question;

2. the one set out like a vast **clock**; the card at each 'hour' representing a month of the coming year with a 13th card in the middle to sum up the year.

It is also useful to adopt the suggestion by Aleister Crowley (celebrated satanist and all-round bad person) that Grand Arcana cards 8 – 'La Justice', and 11 – 'La Force', should be swapped round. To make life difficult he also changed their names to 'Adjustments' and 'Lust'. Calling 'La Force' Lust can fairly brighten up some mundane readings.

Having Fun with the Tarot

As with all fortune telling, Tarot has to be carried off with a totally straight face or it loses all its effect. But this does not mean you cannot have a little bit of innocent fun while reading the cards.

One piece of harmless nonsense, especially useful if you are not totally sympathetic to the person whose cards are being read, is to lay everything out carefully, look at them without a word for four or five minutes and then just pick them up, announcing in a distracted manner that you don't really feel like carrying on at that moment. Then, no matter how often they say 'You saw something in the cards, didn't you? There's something you don't want to tell me?', just appear to be trying to act normally and insist that you just didn't feel like giving a reading. You can boost your reputation to foretell the future no end, without saying a word.

This is a variation on the old trick when you get the Death card No 13. As soon as the querent sees the Grim Reaper just pick up the cards saying "Well not much point going into too much detail about your future, is there?" Hours of fun there.

To be really nasty get the Thoth pack designed by Aleister Crowley, which has huge cards that are just too big to hold. Then tell your victim to shuffle thoroughly but not to drop them as that is desperately bad luck.

Obscurity rating – 4/10
Artistic interpretation – 9/10
Technical merit – 9/10

I CHING

It is well worth studying **I Ching** (The Book of Changes) if only as a practical lesson on how vague and obscure you can be in your predictions and still get away with it. I Ching (pronounced Eeh Jeng, so look condescending if anyone calls it 'eye ching') is thought to be the oldest surviving book in the world, at 2,000 years old, which just goes to show that people have been bluffing for a very long time.

It is based on 64 hexagrams (an arrangement of six broken or unbroken lines) which go under such enlightening names as '**Keeping Still, Mountain**', or '**The Corners of the Mouth**'. Each has a judgement – a series of ambiguous, contradictory and downright confusing sayings that sound like the bits of home-spun philosophy that you get in Kung-Fu films.

For example, say you ask the I Ching "Should I get married?" it might reply *"The Clinging. Perseverance furthers. It brings success. Care of the cow brings good fortune."*

That's what you'd get if you picked hexagram 30 helpfully named **The Clinging Fire**. You might think you were doing better if you got hexagram 51 **The Arousal**, until you read the judgement: *"Shock brings success, Shock comes – oh, oh!, laughing words – ha, ha!, The shock terrifies for a hundred miles, And he does not let fall the sacrificial spoon and chalice."*

The advantage with I Ching is that unlike Tarot or Astrology where it would be bad form to look up a meaning in a book, you are expected to consult the Book of Changes, so you need not commit much to memory.

Each judgement in the book is explained by a commentary which if possible is slightly more confusing than the judgement. It could have been invented by a bluffer.

Of course, you let the querent read the judgement and the commentary himself. When they get to something like *"Six in the fifth place means dense clouds No rain from our western territory, The Prince shoots and hits him who is in the cave"* you will be begged to say what it means and can let your interpretative powers have full rein.

Casting the Hexagram

It is in the method of arriving at the hexagrams that the real skill of I Ching lies. If possible use:

The Yarrow Stalk Method

Take 50 Yarrow stalks and put one between the ring finger and little finger of your left hand. Don't ask why. Just do it. Then split the rest into two bundles and count off the first group in fours. What is left, you put between the ring finger and middle finger of the left hand.

Do the same with the other bundle and put the remainder between the middle finger and the index finger of the left hand. According to the book you will now have either 5 or 9 stalks sticking out from odd places in your fingers, though there is a reasonable chance that you could have anything between three and 47. The first time you do this you ignore the first stalk. So if you have 9 stalks in your hand you count that as 8 and if you have 5 you count that as 4.

This is where it starts to get complicated. If you have 4 stalks, it is regarded as a complete unit which counts as 3, but if you have 8 stalks it is a double unit which of course counts as 2. This isn't a joke. This is the proper way to do it.

Having worked this out with great difficulty the natural thing to do is to put them aside and start again. This time you are supposed to get either 8 or 4, which seems pushing the laws of coincidence just too far. They also end up as 2 or 3. If by some miracle you actually manage to do this, you are then asked to do it one more time. You add the three scores (that's the ones that came out 2 and 3) and this should give you:

a) 9 – the old yang written as o;
b) 8 – the young yin written as a broken line;
c) 7 – the young yang written as an unbroken line; or
d) 6 – the old yin written as x,

each represented by a different kind of line. And that is how to get the first of the six lines of the hexagram.

With us so far? No? Well don't worry. Neither is anyone else, and that includes the experts. In fact the Yarrow Stalk method is one of the all time great bluffs. This is actually a simplified version. The real thing goes on in that vein for three pages and means absolutely nothing. Even renowned I Ching experts don't like to do the Yarrow Stalk method in front of another expert in case they're doing it wrong. It is thus a real must for the bluffer. As long as you carry out your own method with enough assurance, no-one will challenge you.

The Coin Method

If you want to consult the I Ching for real (for those few occasions when you are not actually bluffing) use the coin method. This involves three coins which tradition insists should be old Chinese bronze coins with a hole in the middle and an inscription on one side. Or use the first three coins you can get. (Make sure to pocket them afterwards so at least you make a profit from the reading.) Pick one side as the yin (2) and by a process of elimination the other side becomes the yang (3).

Throw the three coins in the air and count the total of yins and yangs. This tells you what kind of line you have (as above) so you have to do it six times for each hexagram. Look up the correct hexagram and your future is revealed. Unfortunately you won't have a clue what it all means, but that's just a problem you have to face.

Interpretation

It is difficult to give any hard and fast guidance on how to interpret the I Ching although this is no real problem. The experts have been arguing for years about what the words actually are, far less what they mean, so you would be very unlikely to find yourself in the position of being corrected when interpreting.

Here are a few phrases that you see quite regularly and may need to have a pat answer for:

Crossing the Water – A phrase you will find constantly which does not mean going to America (it was written 2,000 years ago so they would really have had to be good at fortune telling to refer to America). It is normally read as "undertaking a great task".

The superior man – Whoever you are consulting the I Ching for.

The inferior man – Whoever you are consulting the I Ching for if they don't listen to your advice.

Perseverance – A word you find in virtually every hexagram of the I Ching and is basic to the whole philosophy.

As you can see, hexagrams all have the same meaning – "Keep plugging away".

Jung and I Ching

Never complete even the simplest I Ching consultation without a mention of Carl Jung and '**synchronicity**'.

The co-founder of modern psychiatry did I Ching the favour of being totally hooked on it. He would consult it over whether to take one or two spoonfuls of sugar in his tea in the morning. Since he used the Yarrow Stalk method, he was used to drinking cold tea.

Being Jung he couldn't do this just because he was superstitious. He had to invent synchronicity, a theory best summed up in the idea that coincidences are just too significant to be just coincidences.

Jung can be used to justify all forms of fortune telling and his interest in I Ching is best known. But don't quote him directly on the Tarot. For some reason this was the only area of rich 'archetypal' symbolism he never wrote about. Just coincidence probably.

Obscurity rating – 8/10
Artistic interpretation – 8/10
Technical merit (using Yarrow Stalks) – 10/10

PALMISTRY

Reading palms is the ideal method for the unmitigated flirt. No other skill allows you to take attractive members of the opposite sex into a quiet corner at a party, hold their hand for 20 minutes and whisper in their ear. And you can do this while their spouse is standing at the other side of the room looking on.

Unfortunately reading palms proves totally fascinating to the most unlikely people. No sooner have you finished the consultation you engineered when some horny-handed farmer will stick his callouses under your nose and insist that you start again. At this moment you will discover that you need more than a good chat-up line to be a palmist.

So first, do not allow anyone to listen while you are reading a palm. This allows you to use the same reading for everyone (with a few minor adjustments). Luckily palmistry is based on rather loose qualitative judgements. For instance you can tell virtually everyone that they have "long fingers showing an artistic temperament" and they will accept it.

Vagueness is used constantly. Say you read a palm where the index and middle fingers are the same length. If you decide that the *index* finger is as long as the middle finger, the querent is dictatorial and self centred, but if the *middle* finger is as long as the index finger, it shows that the querent is intuitive. It would seem difficult to lose out in such a situation.

It is even pretty vague what hand you read. Some systems say the right hand shows the future and the left the past, or the right hand shows the outer character and the left shows the instinctive nature. Best to read the right hand. Then if you say something they don't like they can only hit you with their left.

Technical Terms

At first there would seem to be some minor difficulties to be faced in practising **Cheiromancy** (always talk of "cheiromancy": it's from the Greek so it's much more impressive). For instance, it is an immensely complicated science with slight variations in skin patterns, tiny changes in the shape of finger nails and minute measurements all playing a significant part. It is worth mentioning this to the querent though in reality you totally ignore it.

Palmistry is also one of the most popular and best known forms of fortune telling. Most people have at least a vague idea where their life line or love line is on the palm. As long as it is vague, this helps enormously of course.

There are thousands of technical terms involved. This is a case where it is better to remember the technical terms than to remember what they actually mean. It sounds more impressive to say "My, look at that Mount of Mercury. I've never seen one that size before" than to tell the person that a Mount of Mercury as small as that means they are "dull, gullible and humourless". As long as you can point out each part of the hand and give it a plausible technical term people won't worry too much about what you say it means.

The other reason why it is so popular (especially with bluffers) is that it only *touches* on real prediction. You can get away with really simple stuff like "you will live until you're 80 and have some illness in later life". All very safe. Who's going to come back to you and say "You said I would die at 80 and I actually died at 53"?

More important is that you have to give an accurate

description of the querent's character based on the signs in their hands. People seldom seem to realise that if you've known someone for 20 years you might have some way of assessing their personality other than the shape of their fingers. This is where the technical terms come into their own. For instance, you can explain that you have guessed that the querent has a cold, passionless nature through the fact that their Plain of Venus was underdeveloped, and not because you have been married to them for 15 years.

It is totally useless consulting books on palmistry. They will provide thousands of line drawings showing the position of the lines and mounts and giving examples of shapes of palms, fingers, nails and skin patterns. But as soon as you compare them to a real hand you find you might as well be looking at a llama's hoof. Not once has a real hand come close to an example in a book – a co-incidence that seems significant.

You will spend hours looking for 'The line of sexual attraction' or some other excitingly named line to discover that you just don't have one. Books will tell you there are four 'mounts' running along the top of the palm (bits that stick up). Many people just have three mounts but books never tell you how decide which three you have and therefore which part of your personality is sadly lacking.

The Technique

The best idea is to memorise as many technical terms as you can and just pick a suitable part of the palm to suit the term. The great advantage is that most parts of the hand are named after planets so if you have learnt your **astrological symbolism** you just use the same set for palmistry.

If people know anything about palmistry they know about the lines. You should therefore only pay a passing interest in them. Your real interest is fingers. Each finger has a different function:

Index finger is ruled by Jupiter – career.

Middle finger is ruled by Saturn – fate.

Ring finger is ruled by the Sun (or Apollo) – creativity.

Little finger is ruled by Mercury – intelligence and communications.

Thumb – governs leadership qualities, vitality and the ability to get a lift.

With these facts you can build up an interpretation lasting half an hour on the fingers alone. Whether each finger is straight (lucky) or bent (rugby player), whether it is longer or shorter than the others (more or less important), can also be used to great effect.

Each part of the finger is called a 'phalange' and has its own meaning. Make up your own since not even an expert is likely to remember all of these.

The shape of the fingers and the palm are also important. As general rule the thicker the hand or finger the thicker the querent, the thinner and more slender, the more intelligent. But remember it was clairvoyants who made up the rules. The slenderest hand with the thinnest most graceful fingers belongs not to the genius but to the psychic. Here are a few others worth remembering:

Square palm with short fingers – practical;

Long palm with short fingers – intuitive;

Long palm with long fingers – imaginative;

Square palm with long fingers – intellectual;

Hairy palm with very long fingers – an ability to swing from trees.

Even the shape of the nails is taken into account. Give squat, short nails an earthy, practical reading and long, well-shaped nails more intellectual traits. Very large square nails are supposed to show a cold, selfish nature, and beautifully shaped oval nails show a placid, easy going personality (they are the only ones with time for a manicure).

The Mounts

Next study the mounts on the palm. If you are unsure just pick the biggest mount, name it after a planet and then decide whether it is big, fleshy, small, or firm. This will give you enough of a clue to work out a suitable meaning. For example a flat undeveloped Plain of Venus could signify a cold, detached character while a high, firm one could show that the querent was highly sexed. Most palmists look here first.

Here is a list of some of the mounts with a vague idea of where you might find them.

The Mount of Venus – The fleshy part next to the thumb. This rules romance and passion.

Across the top of the palm (starting at the thumb) are:

The Mount of Jupiter – Enthusiasm and career.

The Mount of Saturn – Discipline and a serious attitude to life (probably missing on all good bluffers).

The Mount of the Sun – A happy nature.

The Mount of Mercury – The arts and the ability to communicate.

Just below this on the heel of the hand are:

The Mount of Mars – The aggressive side of your nature.

The Mount of the Moon – Yes. Intuition again.

The Lines

By the time you have gone round all the mounts you won't really need to go into too much detail about the lines. The books all give you 20 lines to look for. Ignore this. Just remember four names and pick a suitable line to fit.

The Life Line – *Curls round the base of the thumb*. Everyone knows this one. It tells how long you will live, any illnesses and major events affecting your life. The time scale starts at the top and gets to your wrist about the age of 70. Just look for any chains, breaks or twists and interpret these as important events.

The Love Line – *Horizontal, starting at the little finger side, across the top of the palm.* This is also very popular as it tells about the love life. Chaining shows a flirt and all the loops and breaks show affairs and divorces. Hours of fun with this one.

The Head Line – *Horizontal below the love line.* This shows the level of intellect. A good bluffer checks this one out to see how much he can get away with.

The Fate Line – *Running up the middle of the palm.* This shows how fate will play a part in your life. No fate line means a smooth and uneventful life. Have a look. You will find yours is deep and twisted.

If anyone finds a line on their palm that you haven't mentioned and says something like "Hey what about this one that you're ignoring then, smarty?" just make it "the Line of Unwarranted Scepticism" or "the Line of Doubting Thomas" which shows "a pathetic desire to cling to outmoded beliefs because a limited intellect cannot grasp the truth".

As well as interpreting from the shape and consistency of the line, you can use the fact of where the line starts and finishes to bring in other details. So if your lifeline starts at your Mount of Jupiter, life will be successful but if it starts at the Mount of Saturn, life will be a struggle. And if the Life Line crosses the Line of Unwarranted Scepticism the person is in danger of meeting an early and painful death – probably at the hands of a palmist.

Obscurity rating – 2/10
Artistic interpretation – 7/10
Technical merit – 4/10

RUNES

It is said that Odin, the father of the Norse gods, hanged himself by the neck from Yggdrasil (the World Ash Tree which supported heaven, earth and the underworld) for nine days, impaled on his own spear, in order to snatch the **Runes** from the Norns, the three female guardians of the tree and gain the knowledge of how to use them. He must have been sick to discover that you can buy them by mail order complete with a velveteen carrying bag and a book of instructions.

Runes look really impressive. They are 22 small pieces of stone or wood each with a totally indecipherable symbol etched on it. These are the letters of the Norse alphabet. For some reason you always 'cast' the runes although there is no actual casting involved. Anyone who does try to throw your Runes about should be invited to leave. Instead you lay them out face down, shuffle them about like dominoes and ask the querent to pick 13.

Place 12 of these in a circle like a clock (though you read them anti-clockwise). Each place has its own distinctive meaning, all the usual ones you know about already – number 2, money matters; number 7, love and marriage; number 10, career; and number 13 goes in the middle to tell you the final outcome.

You look at each Rune in turn, give its interpretation, tying it in with the runes on either side and opposite. The Runes can be upright or reversed (reversed is unlucky). They each give simple messages like 'Plan ahead' or 'Beware of accidents'.

The experienced bluffer will of course have immediately spotted a few basic problems. If you don't happen to know the Norse alphabet it is impossible to tell one

Rune from another, far less whether it is upright or not. Even if you tie the 22 runes in with another system (both Astrology and the Tarot have been suggested), it is still a major feat of memory to remember each obscure symbol. They are not even numbered to allow you to use a numerological system.

On the other hand there is very little traditional information about Runes and everything written today seems to be based on information revealed clairvoyantly to people living in Glastonbury. This means that a master bluffer who is prepared to invest a little time and imagination could work out his or her own system (all revealed clairvoyantly of course), write a book about it and absolutely no-one would be able to dispute a word of it. Or else you could hang from the tree Yggdrasil for nine days.

Obscurity rating – 11/10
Artistic interpretation – 0/10
Technical merit – 10/10

ONEIROMANCY

Oneiromancy (pronounced 'On-eye-romancy'), and also known as **Oneirocriticism**, covers the dark and mysterious subject of dreams – a fascinating twilight world of intuition and suggestion – a natural area of interest to the bluffer. Everyone dreams. If you think you don't dream it's because you can't remember dreaming (reasonable enough – you're asleep at the time).

However, it is now scientifically proved that if you didn't dream over an extended period you would hallucinate and eventually go mad. You don't need to admit this to anyone though.

You can make a fabulous reputation for yourself by staring searchingly into the eyes of someone who claims never to dream and saying "You will dream tonight". If you say it with enough authority you will put the idea into their head and that night they may remember their dreams.

Dreams are totally fascinating but usually only to the person who had the dream – a fact the good bluffer can use to great effect. Most people will be pathetically grateful just to be given the chance to talk about their dreams and if you can then go on to tell them what it means, you have them eating out of your hand.

Yet there are few Oneirocritics about – always use the word 'Oneirocritic' instead of 'Oneiromancer'. Any word containing the word 'romancer' makes it sound too much as if you are making it all up.

It would seem very much a specialist art. This is simply because people can dream about thousands of different things. Look at any book on dreams and it's like a dictionary with pages of dream themes each with a short explanation: for example 'Aardvark – to dream of an aardvark means you will receive a message from a close relative'.

There is absolutely no point in trying to pass yourself off as an Oneirocritic by reading out these comments from the book. People would quickly get the idea and buy the book themselves. So you instantly have to be able to take any dream subject and give an authoritative interpretation. This is no problem when you know how.

Interpretation

All you need to do is to apply the following rules:

1. Accept that you will never remember interpretations for all the possible subjects and instead develop a method of consistently producing some likely sounding meaning. Decide on a policy: for instance, all references to animals have to do with career moves or all dreams about fish are about your sex life – and stick to it.

2. Ask lots of very detailed questions about the dream. Never let them say "I dreamt about a cow". Always ask what kind of cow it was. Was it in a field? Was it fat or thin? Was it beef or dairy? Never mind if you can't think of any significance to the fact that it was a thin Ayrshire in the middle of the Stock Exchange. The mere fact that you have asked all these questions makes it look as if you have a specific interpretation for each answer.

3. Pick out something as being particularly significant. For instance you could insist on knowing the colour of everything in the dream. Then you could have a simple colour code to give you an idea to hang your interpretation on, e.g., green = intuition or fruitfulness; red = passion or sinfulness, black = evil, blue = purity, pale puce = an overfanciful imagination. Statistics show that most people (especially men) dream a lot in black and white so you can cover yourself nicely if a prediction is proved wrong.

4. Have pat answers for dreams of the things people commonly dream about: parts of the body, journeys, etc. They are liable to ask you about the same dream

twice so you don't want to be caught out being inconsistent. Keep them simple and easy to remember. For instance dreaming about your ears could mean you were going to get some news. But still ask all the questions. For example sore ears could mean bad news or cauliflower ears would mean that you have to be sceptical about what you heard.

5. Throw in a few totally illogical interpretations. This is widely used by the professionals. For instance dreaming of a sore stomach is traditionally interpreted as a sign of good health, dreaming of an amputation means a useful gain, and dreaming of your own death means a change for the better. Maybe they know something we don't know.

6. Never make your interpretations too obvious. Think obliquely. For instance if you are faced with a dream about falling off a roof the immediate inclination is to predict disaster. The proper interpretation is "a temporary success". It's obvious when you think about it: you'll succeed in staying alive until you hit the ground. The traditional meaning given to dreaming about being a different sex is "an improvement for the better". They obviously know something we don't.

7. Never give an interpretation just on one symbol. Get six or seven and then build them into a little story. You don't dry up so easily that way and it is far more difficult for the querent to remember all the details and thus catch you out at a later date.

Obscurity rating – 7/10
Artistic interpretation – 9/10
Technical merit – 3/10

PHRENOLOGY

Feeling bumps sounds really interesting until you realise that the only bumps you are allowed to feel are the ones on the skull.

If you have ever described someone as an 'egg-head' you are already well on the way to being an expert in the esoteric art of **Phrenology**. The ovoid or 'egg' shaped skull is supposed to signify an intellectual nature. A round head shows a positive but restless nature and the faithful old square head shows a solid, reliable personality.

The main advantage of the science, according to dedicated phrenologists, is that it helps you tell an idiot (no forehead) from a genius (lots and lots of forehead). You can't help feeling there are more obvious ways of telling.

Like palmistry it is complicated, with over 40 tiny areas on each side of the head to be taken into account. If you find a bump in a specific area it shows a capacity or a personality trait. It is, of course, totally impossible to remember them, and even the experts could not tell whether a bump is in the area of **Combativeness** (an ability to punch someone's head in) or fractions of an inch away in **Conjugality** (an ability to be faithful in love and the desire to get married).

You can use a bit of pseudo-science by talking at length about the different hemispheres of the brain. In phrenology the areas of interest are duplicated on both sides of the skull so if you find a bump on one side of the head and not on the other you can make great play of it. The left side of the brain deals with speech and reasoning while the right side deals with spatial awareness. Find the **Benevolence** bump on the left side of the skull (generosity) but not on the right side and you could suggest that person talks a lot about being generous but their hand cannot find its way to their pocket.

Interpretation

Have a set number of favourite bumps with a vague idea of their position and then find a suitable bump to fit the bill. As with palmistry, do each reading in private. It would seem just too much of a coincidence if everyone at the party had the same qualities.

Here are a few suggestions.

Adhesiveness – *Around the back somewhere.*
Apparently to do with an ability to make friends and to be sociable, although with that name you could be forgiven for suggesting "a tendency to come to a sticky end".

Amativeness – *Base of the skull.*
The ability to appeal to the opposite sex (it is well worth finding this on everyone except for a few obvious exceptions).

Alimentativeness – *Just above the ear.*
A liking for food (this should be pretty obvious without finding a bump).

Benevolence – *Top of the head towards the front.*
Generosity (if you are being paid for the reading it is important to find this).

Humanity – Top, middle of the forehead. It might

seem surprising that phrenologists need this one because you would think that most would be able to tell pretty quickly whether or not the head they were fondling belonged to a human as opposed to, say, a sacred donkey. However, it seems to be more about the subjects' ability to judge the character of other humans.

Individuality – *Middle of the forehead.*
An inquisitive mind (beware of this one, just in case it's true and they see through you).

Languages – *Under the eye.*
An ability to learn foreign languages and eloquence.

Order – *Beside the eyebrow.*
The desire to be systematic and organised.

Philoprogentiveness – *Lower back of the skull.*
Parental love and care for the less fortunate (not really very interesting as a bump but worth using just for the name).

Phrenology generally tends towards being complimentary. The bumps usually denote a positive ability or skill. However you don't need to stick to this if you feel like finding a spurious bump that makes the person "inclined to say silly things" or gives them "a desire to cheat at Trivial Pursuits".

Obscurity rating – 7/10
Artistic interpretation – 3/10
Technical merit – 7/10

METOPOSCOPY

If you are going to read bumps and palms you might as well dabble in **Metoposcopy**, reading the lines on the forehead. (There is also Physiognomy, reading the shape of the face and features but that's just silly.)

Metoposcopy was invented by Jerome Cardan (1501-1576), the eminent mathematician who was the first person to write about the mathematics of chance and probability. Cardan was also an astrologer and is thought to have starved himself to death just to prove that his astrological prediction for his death was correct.

This is, of course, quite the daftest prediction anyone can make as you gain no benefit at all from being right. If you are tempted to do anything as foolhardy make sure to predict that you will die at the age of 120. If you're right it will be amazing, and if you're wrong, what does it matter.

Metoposcopy is one of the silliest occult sciences you can indulge in and probably no-one has used it since 1576 when Cardan died. This of course makes it ideal for bluffers. Another advantage is that it is heavily based on **astrological symbolism** so if you have learnt your planets, you are already a Metoposcopist.

To carry it out you have to divide the forehead into seven equal parts. You could do this with a ruler and a black felt tip pen (not recommended) or you could take a wild guess presuming that no-one knows enough to prove you wrong (recommended). Each section is ruled by one of seven old planets. Luckily the science was evolved before the three new planets were found or there wouldn't have been room to move on some foreheads.

The sections are (from the top):

Saturn – caution and discipline.

Jupiter – career and good fortune.

Mars – courage and aggression.

Sun – worldly success.

Venus – love and romance.

Mercury – humour and eloquence.

Moon – intuition and imagination.

Any lines below this, are the eyebrows.

You then look to see if there is a straight, clear line (good) or a broken line (bad). In each section, compare the length of the lines and the direction they curve and take conclusions from that. For instance if the line of Mercury is long and deep (humour) and curls away from the line of Venus (love) you can conclude that the person does not find their love life funny.

Cardan went further and produced drawings to show typical foreheads that showed 'a man destined to die by a head wound' or 'a poisoner'. Somehow this list does not seem to be as useful now as it was in Cardan's time.

Obscurity rating – 10/10
Artistic interpretation – 2/10
Technical merit – 4/10

MOLESCOPY

Molescopy is divination by means of moles (brown marks on the skin, not the creatures that dig up your lawn). Although this is not really a serious method of augury, it can be used to create an instant impression and could produce hours of innocent fun looking for skin blemishes in more and more unlikely places.

Moles on the face are obviously the most useful. For instance, you can tell a complete stranger that because he has a mole on his right temple he is exceptionally able but should guard against illness in later life. Don't however try it with someone who has a mole in the middle of their forehead. This is supposed to show a vicious nature and a bad temper. It could just be true.

Here is a short list of where it is most fun to find moles.

Bridge of the nose – Lust (one to look out for).

Nose left side – Untrustworthy (get your money in advance).

Eyebrow – While they will be happy in marriage they should beware of food poisoning and being hit by lightning. Perhaps the mole could be used to attach a lightning conductor.

Finger – Dishonest, prone to exaggerate (cover yours up with a plaster if you want to mention this one).

Nipple – A flirty type.

Navel – Great good fortune.

Abdomen – Voracious and self-indulgent. The bearer is advised to marry someone placid. Anyone placid is advised to steer clear.

Buttock – A total lack of ambition.

Loins – Overamorous (could be interesting proving this one).

Small of the back – A good liar.

General Rules

Side of the body
If the mole is on the right side of the body it is something good and on the left side it is something bad (except for the arms where for some reason this is reversed).

Colour
The darker the mole, the worse the reading.

Shape
The shape is also important if a bit confusing. An oval mole is bad luck while an oblong mole is great good fortune. Anyone who can tell the difference should send their answers on the back of a £10 note to Bluffer's Guides®.

Obscurity rating – 9/10
Artistic interpretation – 3/10
Technical merit – 6/10

GEOMANCY

Though used all over the world, **Geomancy** was once a very popular method in Arabia where geomancers made predictions by throwing a handful of sand on the ground and interpreting the patterns it made. (If you had the Sahara next door this would be less expensive than having to provide a cupful of tea-leaves.)

Simply throw some dust, powder or sand on the floor and look to see if it falls into any shape that seems meaningful to you. Or spread it, make some marks in it (by letting your hand move "as it wills according to the dictates of your unconscious"), then decide what the marks mean. Interestingly, these are all techniques widely used by three-year-olds at play-school.

Stick to simple marks – squiggles, lines, circles, tetrahedrons (well, maybe not tetrahedrons) – and then decide what they look like. If they look like the letter 'n' the answer is no. Anything like a 'y' and it's a yes. A 'p' could be perhaps and and 'm' maybe, which you might feel is not the sort of answer someone who has proffered hard cash to seek guidance on a crucial question would be totally happy with.

A long straight line would represent a journey (there should be a few of them in each reading); crosses mean arguments, and bird means news – a seagull-like squiggle, not a line-drawing of a hen harrier in flight. No matter how tempted you are to save time you should never let your marks look anything like the words 'received with thanks, £50'.

Obscurity rating – 9/10
Artistic merit – 10/10
Technical merit – 1/10

THE AUTHOR

Alexander C. Rae is going to be a world famous author and will win the Booker Prize, though he is going to be pipped at the post for a Nobel Prize for Literature. He will live to the ripe old age of 98 when it looks likely he will die in an unfortunate sky-diving accident.

His Ascendant is in conjunction with the Sun in Gemini in his natal chart which makes him a brilliant writer and in Chinese Astrology he is a Metal Tiger which makes him forceful, creative, warm and cuddly. He is married to a Dragon and has two children, a Monkey and a Rat. He also has two dogs and a cat, one born in the Year of the Llama and the other two born in the Year of the Gerbil.

He has a long psychic palm and long, tapering, artistic fingers, a mole on his right cheek which proves he will be successful, and his bumps need to be felt to be believed.